THE COUNTRYSIDE

LIFE IN VICTORIAN ENGLAND

THE COUNTRYSIDE

VIRGINIA SCHOMP

MARSHALL CAVENDISH · BENCHMARK
NEW YORK

For Barbara Pezzella

The author and publishers would like to thank Walter L. Arnstein, Professor of History Emeritus at the University of Illinois at Urbana-Champaign, for his valuable comments and careful reading of the manuscript.

Other Marshall Cavendish Offices: Marshall Cavendish International (Asia) Private Limited, 1 New Industrial Road, Singapore 536196 • Marshall Cavendish International (Thailand) Co Ltd. 253 Asoke, 12th Flr, Sukhumvit 21 Road, Klongtoey Nua, Wattana, Bangkok 10110, Thailand • Marshall Cavendish (Malaysia) Sdn Bhd, Times Subang, Lot 46, Subang Hi-Tech Industrial Park, Batu Tiga, 40000 Shah Alam, Selangor Darul Ehsan, Malaysia

Marshall Cavendish is a trademark of Times Publishing Limited
All websites were available and accurate when this book was sent to press.

LIBRARY OF CONGRESS CATALOGING-IN-PUBLICATION DATA Schomp, Virginia. The countryside / Virginia Schomp.p. cm. — (Life in Victorian England) Includes bibliographical references and index. Summary: "Describes daily life in the countryside of England during the reign of Queen Victoria (1837-1901), from the poor, to the middle classes, to the upper classes"—Provided by publisher. ISBN 978-1-60870-030-1 1. Country life—England—History—19th century—Juvenile literature. 2. England—Social life and customs—19th century—Juvenile literature. 3. Great Britain—History—Victoria, 1837-1901—Juvenile literature. 4. Villages—England—History—19th century—Juvenile literature. 5. Farm life—England—History—19th century—Juvenile literature. I. Title. DA533.S36 2010 941.081—dc22 2010006902

EDITOR: Joyce Stanton PUBLISHER: Michelle Bisson ART DIRECTOR: Anahid Hamparian SERIES DESIGNER: Michael Nelson

Images provided by Rose Corbett Gordon, Art Editor of Mystic CT, from the following sources: Cover: Fine Art Photographic Library, London/ Art Resource, NY Back cover: The Francis Frith Collection/ Art Resource, NY Pages 1,21: The Francis Frith Collection/Art Resource, NY; pages 2-3,11,18,26,40,41,50: Fine Art Photographic Library, London/Art Resource, NY; page 7: The Art Archive/Lincoln Museum and Gallery/Eileen Tweedy; page 8: The Art Archive/Lynette Hemmant; page 12: The Art Archive/Private Collection/Marc Charmet; page 13: The Art Archive/Private Collection/Eileen Tweedy; page 15: Art Resource, NY; page 22: Ashmolean Museum, University of Oxford/Bridgeman Art Library; page 23: Victoria & Albert Museum/Art Resource, NY; page 25: NMPFT/RPS/SSPL/The Image Works; page 28: Royal Pavilion, Libraries & Museums, Brighton & Hove/Bridgeman Art Library; page 31: Charles Young Fine Paintings, London/Bridgeman Art Library; page 34: Private Collection/Bridgeman Art Library; pages 36,46,66: Mary Evans Picture Library/The Image Works; page 43: NMPFT/SSPL/The Image Works; page 44: Tate, London/Art Resource, NY; page 48: The Fine Art Society, London/,Bridgeman Art Library, © Courtesy of the Sir George Clausen Estate; page 51: Usher Gallery, Lincolnshire/Bridgeman Art Library; page 53: Private Collection/Bourne Gallery/Bridgeman Art Library; page 55: SSPL/Getty Images; page 56: NMPFT/Kodak Collection/SSPL/The Image Works; page 58: Graham Reed Fine Art, York/Bridgeman Art Library; page 61: ARPL/HIP/The Image Works; page 62: The Print Collector/HIP/The Image Works; page 69: The Art Archive/Sotheby's/Eileen Tweedy; page 70: Fine Art Photographic Library/Corbis.

Printed in Malaysia (T)
135642

Front cover: The Return of the Gleaners by Victorian artist Myles Birket Foster
Half-title page: Two well-to-do Victorian children and their pups
Title page: The Shepherd's Daughter by English landscape artist William Kay Blacklock
Back cover: Twin girls in Whitby, a fishing village on the northeast coast of England

CONTENTS

ABOUT VICTORIAN ENGLAND

On June 20, 1837, King William IV of England died, and his eighteen-year-old niece, Victoria, ascended the throne. The teenage queen recorded her thoughts in her diary:

> Since it has pleased Providence to place me in this station, I shall do my utmost to fulfil my duty towards my country; I am very young and perhaps in many, though not in all things, inexperienced, but I am sure, that very few have more real good will and more real desire to do what is fit and right than I have.

That blend of faith, confidence, devotion to duty, and the earnest desire to do good would guide Victoria through the next sixty-three years and seven months, the longest reign of any English monarch. The queen's personal qualities would also set the tone for the period that bears her name, the Victorian Age.

Today the term *Victorian* is sometimes used to describe someone who is prim and prudish. We may think of Queen Victoria as a stuffy old lady presiding over a long, formal dinner party where everyone watches their language and worries about which fork to use. That image is not entirely wrong. Victoria and her subjects *did* believe in "traditional values" such as duty, discipline, and self-control. Their society *was* governed by a set of strict moral and social rules. However, that is not the whole picture. When we look deeper, we discover that the Victorian era, far from being dull and predictable, was a period of extraordinary change. Between 1837 and 1901, England was transformed from a mostly agricultural, isolated society into a modern industrial nation with territories all over the world. The Victorian people witnessed astonishing advances in science and tech-

A farmer and his prize sheep. Victorian farmers competed to breed the largest farm animals, with the most meat or wool.

nology, as well as sweeping political, legal, and social reforms. A Victorian physician named Sir Henry Holland described his exciting times as "an age of transition, a period when changes, deeply and permanently affecting the whole condition of mankind, are occurring more rapidly, as well as extensively, than at any prior time in human history."

Life in Victorian England takes a look at this dynamic era, with a focus on the people and their everyday lives. The four books in the series will introduce us to men, women, and children at all levels of society, from poor farmers and factory workers to striving middle-class families to the aristocrats at the top of the social scale. In this volume we will meet the squires, farmers, laborers, and craftspeople who lived in the Victorian countryside. We will see where these people lived and worked, how they celebrated special occasions, and how they coped with the challenges of their times.

Now it is time to step back to a world that is poised on the brink of the modern age. Welcome to an era when gas lamps are giving way to electric lightbulbs, stagecoaches to locomotives, wooden sailing vessels to iron warships. Welcome to life in Victorian England!

A timeless country scene—but beneath the tranquil surface, the Victorian country-side was changing.

ONE

A CHANGING WORLD

It is part and parcel of the wide-spread social changes
which have gradually been proceeding. . . .
The civilization of the town has, in fact, gone out
and taken root afresh in the country.
⁓RICHARD JEFFERIES, *HODGE AND HIS MASTERS* (1880)

THE VICTORIAN AGE SAW THE RAPID RISE OF INDUSTRY and the great industrial centers that would become the world's first modern cities. Meanwhile, far from the crowded city streets and noisy factories, the lives of millions of people continued to revolve around agriculture. When Victoria took the throne in 1837, about two-thirds of her subjects lived in the countryside and one in every five families depended on farming for a living. By 1851, the great migration of country dwellers to towns and cities was under way. Even so, nearly half the population still lived in rural areas, and the largest single group of wage earners still worked in agriculture.

Books and paintings often portray country life as quiet and unchanging. That picture bears little resemblance to rural England under the reign of Queen Victoria. While much of the action in these dynamic decades was centered in the cities, the Victorian period also transformed the lives of country dwellers, sometimes for the better, sometimes for the worse.

THE "AGRICULTURAL REVOLUTION"

The transformation of country life began several decades before the Victorian era. In the mid- to late 1700s, rapid advances in technology revolutionized the way goods were produced and distributed. Around the same time as this "Industrial Revolution," fundamental changes were also taking place in age-old systems of farming. The "agricultural revolution" would make it possible for farmers to produce more of the food needed to feed England's growing population.

One important force behind the agricultural revolution was the enclosure of farm fields. For centuries villages in many parts of England had been surrounded by large open expanses of land. The wealthy owners of these lands divided their fertile fields into strips, which they rented out to tenant farmers. Scattered among the long strips of farmland were "common lands." All the people of the village had the right to use these parts of the landowner's property for specific purposes: grazing their livestock in the common meadows; gathering fuel in the common woodlands; foraging for nuts, berries, greens, and mushrooms in the common woods, meadows, and marshes. Over time, however, landowners began to enclose their properties. They put up fences, hedges, and stone walls, combining all their scattered strips of farmland into large, uninterrupted farms. A series of laws passed by Parliament in the late eighteenth and early nineteenth centuries accelerated the enclosure process. By the mid-1800s, there was little common land left for the average villager to use.

Enclosure had a number of benefits. A large enclosed farm could be worked more efficiently than many separate strips of land. Large farmers could experiment with the improved farming methods that were being developed by scientists and agricultural experts, such as new systems of crop rotation to improve the soil. Many landowners cleared their woodlands and drained their marshes to bring even more fields under cultivation. Some invested their rising profits in new laborsaving machines, including the mechanical seed drill for planting, steam-powered reapers for harvesting, and threshing machines for separating the harvested grain from the husks and stalks. All these developments revolutionized English agriculture, allowing farms to produce more food with fewer workers.

At the same time, the agricultural revolution caused hardships for some less prosperous people. Some small landowners were forced to sell their holdings because they could not afford to enclose or

The estates of wealthy aristocrats included miles and miles of rolling hills, meadows, woods, and farmland.

An ad for Walter Wood's self-raking reaper, one of the new farm machines that transformed agriculture in the Victorian Age.

develop them. Some farm laborers lost their jobs to machines. Many poor villagers lost access to the common lands they had relied on to supplement their food supply.

Throughout the Victorian Age, landless villagers would leave the countryside, heading for towns and cities at home and abroad. By 1901, less than one-quarter of the population of England and Wales still lived in rural areas. Historians once thought that the enclosure of common lands was responsible for this great migration. Today many scholars believe that country dwellers left their homes for a variety of reasons, including poor wages and living conditions, a lack of job opportunities, and the rigid class system that ruled over every aspect of rural society. Those same factors would make life a continuous struggle for the people who remained behind.

LANDOWNERS, TENANTS, AND LABORERS

All of Victorian society was divided into classes, but nowhere were these social distinctions more evident than in the small world of the village. In the late 1800s, the English labor leader Joseph Arch described the three levels of rural society: "The squire . . . lorded it . . . over his tenants, the farmers; the farmers in their turn tyrannized over the labourers; the labourers were no better than toads under a harrow."

Nearly all the land in England was owned by a few thousand wealthy people. Richest of all were the titled aristocrats, whose great estates might sweep over 10,000 acres or more. The gentry or "squires," who inherited land but no formal titles, held estates aver-

The squire's grand manor house reflected his lofty standing in country society.

aging from 1,000 to 3,000 acres. Owning land on such a grand scale brought many rewards. Members of the landed classes enjoyed a very comfortable lifestyle, made possible largely by the rents collected from their tenants. They were the undisputed leaders of local government and society. Aristocrats also played a leading role in the national government, although their power would gradually decline throughout the century as the middle class grew in size, wealth, and influence.

Below the landed classes were the farmers. In the Victorian Age, the great majority of farmers were tenants who rented parcels of land from wealthy landowners. The most prosperous tenant farmers, sometimes called "gentlemen farmers," employed large numbers of laborers to work their farms, which might extend over 500 acres or more. Small farmers worked alongside their laborers on farms that were sometimes no larger than 20 acres. Along with the farmers, the middle rung of the social ladder also included the craftsmen and tradesmen who played a vital role in country communities.

At the bottom of rural society were the laborers and farm servants. In 1851 there were more than 1.5 million farm laborers in England and Wales, working for about 250,000 farmers. "Regular laborers" such as plowmen, shepherds, and milkers were hired by the year. "Casual laborers" were hired by the "piece," or job, for short-term tasks such as clearing fields, weeding, and harvesting. Some casual workers moved from farm to farm in large labor gangs under the direction of a foreman or gangmaster. The gangs filled out a farm's workforce at especially busy times such as the harvest, working at a price arranged between the farmer and gangmaster.

Although wages varied from time to time and place to place, farm laborers were nearly always the poorest, most downtrodden people in the countryside. They worked long hours at backbreaking tasks,

THE "DIVINE" SOCIAL ORDER

The class system was such a fundamental part of rural society that some Victorians regarded it as divinely created. Flora Thompson, who grew up in a village in southeast England, later wrote about its strictly ordered world of landowners, farmers, and laborers. Here Flora recalls a sermon by a clergyman whose "favourite subject was the supreme rightness of the social order."

God, in His infinite wisdom, had appointed a place for every man, woman, and child on this earth and it was their bounden duty to remain contentedly in their niches. A gentleman might seem to some of his listeners to have a pleasant, easy life, compared to theirs at field labour; but he had his duties and responsibilities, which would be far beyond their capabilities. He had to pay taxes, sit on the Bench of Magistrates [judges], oversee his estate, and keep up his position by entertaining. Could they do these things? No. Of course they could not; and he [the clergyman] did not suppose that a gentleman could cut as straight a furrow or mow or thatch a rick [haystack] as expertly as they could. So let them be thankful and rejoice in their physical strength and the bounty of the farmer, who found them work on his land and paid them wages with his money.

Above: The lord and lady of the manor

in return for meager wages. A man who toiled with a labor gang for the whole growing season might save barely enough to support his family through the winter. His wife and children usually worked, too. Their wages helped the family survive in a world of grinding poverty and little or no hope of advancement.

VANISHING TRADITIONS

Despite the inequalities in rural society, there was a sense of shared purpose among the people of different social classes. The prosperity of the landed aristocrats and gentry depended on the successful efforts of their tenant farmers. The farmers' success was built on the hard work of their laborers. The village craftsmen supplied the tools needed in the smooth running of the farms and, in turn, relied on the farmers to buy their products.

The closing decades of the nineteenth century witnessed the gradual erosion of these traditional relationships. Village craftsmen saw their livelihoods shrink as machine-made products began to replace handcrafted wares. Tenant farmers struggled through an agricultural depression brought on by cheap imports of foreign foods and several years of bad harvests. During the worst of the depression years, from the late 1870s to the mid-1890s, some farmers converted cropland to livestock pastures, while others gave up farming completely. Many farmers economized by laying off laborers or cutting their wages. Despite these setbacks, farm laborers actually saw their living standards rise toward the end of the century. Lower food prices made it easier to feed their families, while the continuing migration from the countryside forced farmers to treat the remaining workers with greater consideration.

The agricultural depression also had an impact on the landed classes. Many landowners lost income as they reduced rents to help their struggling tenants. Some put unprofitable farmland to new uses such as mining, quarrying, or brick making. Others were forced to sell their estates. Rural mansions that had been in aristocratic families for generations became second homes for newly rich businessmen and industrialists.

All these upheavals in rural society happened more quickly in some areas than others. Throughout the Victorian period, there were many country places where the old ways of life endured. In these scattered villages, the squire in his grand country house still lorded it over the farmer in his farmhouse and the laborer in his small thatched cottage.

Pretty thatched cottages line a winding lane in this romantic painting of a Victorian village.

TWO

The VICTORIAN VILLAGE

> We went on by a pretty little orchard . . .
> to the house itself—a cottage, quite a rustic cottage of doll's rooms;
> but such a lovely place, so tranquil and so beautiful,
> with such a rich and smiling country spread around it.
> —CHARLES DICKENS, *BLEAK HOUSE* (1851–1853)

A JOURNEY ACROSS ENGLAND WOULD SHOW US A GREAT variety of landscapes: rugged mountains and plateaus, rolling hills, fertile valleys, thick forests, boggy marshes, tall white cliffs and sandy beaches on the sea. The diversity of natural features, soil, and climate led to many different kinds of rural settlements. Villages in upland and forested regions tended to be small and scattered. In the more fertile lowlands, men, women, and children labored in the farm fields of great estates.

The nineteenth century brought even more variety to the rural environment. In most of England, enclosure gobbled up the remaining open fields, but in a few areas, large expanses of common land remained. Some country communities were thrust into the industrial age as coal mines or factories sprang up in their midst. Elsewhere life continued to revolve around farming. Despite all these variations, there were broad similarities in the way villages were organized and in the dwellings occupied by people of the different classes.

DOWN A WINDING LANE

There were two basic kinds of Victorian villages: open and closed. Closed villages (also called estate villages) developed under the watchful eye of a resident squire or aristocrat. An open village grew up on its own, on land divided among many owners.

Some open villages took root on the outskirts of growing towns, as squatters settled on patches of land that no one else had claimed. Some were built on common lands by groups of small dairy farmers or craftsmen. Open villages were generally large, straggling communities. The builders threw together new housing whenever and however they saw fit. Flora Thompson recalled her father describing their small squatters' village as "the spot God made with the left-overs when He'd finished creating the rest of the earth."

In contrast, most closed villages were small and well planned. The resident squire owned nearly all the land, and he kept a tight rein on new building. Many picturesque estate villages nestled outside the grounds of the squire's manor house. Elsewhere the buildings might cluster around a village green, often the only trace left of the common lands that had once been open to all villagers.

If we could walk down the stone-and-gravel lane of a Victorian estate village, we would pass neat rows of cottages, each with its own small garden. Our stroll takes us past the shops of the blacksmith, shoemaker, and carpenter. We peer through the window of the general store, where the shelves overflow with bread, cheese, tea, shoes, ribbons, and other goods. We might stop in at the white-washed country

inn, where the men of the village gather for drinks, games, and gossip. Or we might ramble up the hill to a little country church with a low white steeple. From the hilltop we look out over golden fields of grain and an old stone farmhouse. In the distance is the grand manor house, symbol of the wealth, power, and influence of the landed classes.

The estate village of Erlestoke, around 1900. A wealthy squire designed the entire village, adding picturesque cottages along the main street.

THE MANOR HOUSE

The country house of a squire or aristocrat "should always form part of a village," advised the Scottish landscape architect John Claudius Loudon, but it should be "placed, if possible, on rather higher ground." That way the house might "appear to be a sort of head and protector of the surrounding dwellings of the poor."

The landowner's lofty status was reflected not just in his home's location but also in its size and elegance. Manor houses were often as grand and imposing as medieval castles, bristling with towers, domes, and ornamental chimneys. There might be dozens of large rooms: the "great hall," drawing room, library, dining room, breakfast room, morning room, billiard room, smoking room, portrait gallery, a study for the master, a dressing room for the mistress, a nursery

This tastefully furnished drawing room is designed to reflect the family's wealth while creating a warm, comfortable atmosphere.

and schoolroom for the children, and as many as twenty or thirty bedrooms for guests and family members.

Servants spent much of their time in a separate wing of the house and in a variety of outbuildings. Along with the servants' quarters and dining hall, there were special offices for the housekeeper and butler, a huge kitchen, a pantry for dry goods, a larder for meat and fish, a dairy, bakery, brewery, wine cellar, scullery (for washing dishes), laundry, coach house, and stables. Most country houses had at least ten servants, and the grandest might have as many as fifty. These included not only the indoor staff but also the gamekeeper, gardeners, and others who watched over the lawns, parks, and gardens that surrounded the "big house."

FARMHOUSE AND FARMYARD

The farmhouse came with the land that the tenant farmer rented from the squire or aristocrat. Farmers generally held their land for a period of six months or a year, renegotiating their agreement with the landowner each time it expired. Many landowners allowed farmers to pass on their holdings to a son or widow, so that farms often remained in the same family for generations.

The homes of wealthy "gentlemen farmers" were not much different from the squire's manor house. Older farmhouses were usually built of local materials such as wood or stone, while more modern mansions might be constructed from brick and slate. Many of these newer houses boasted a fashionable parlor, drawing room, dining room, and library. When the French historian Hippolyte Taine toured the English countryside in 1862, he was amazed to see a large farmhouse with "a cool and lofty drawing-room. Long curtains held back by gilt [golden] loops; two elegantly framed looking-glasses; chairs in good taste. . . . In short, the country drawing-room of a [wealthy] Parisian."

Most farmhouses were not quite so grand. The home of a reasonably well-off farmer might be designed as two houses in one, with the front holding the living quarters and the back fitted with work spaces such as the dairy and brewery. Small farmers sometimes lived in ramshackle houses little better than a laborer's cottage.

The interior of a cottage or small farmhouse was far less grand than the fine rooms of the manor house.

Farm buildings varied, too. On less prosperous Victorian farms, the buildings looked much as they had decades earlier: a large wooden barn, a hayloft or haystacks, old-fashioned open-sided stalls for the cattle. More up-to-date farms were dotted with stone or brick storage sheds and enclosed animal shelters. The most modern buildings of all were found on the "model farms." In the 1850s and 1860s, during an era known as "high farming," wealthy and innovative landowners delighted in building model farms that showcased the latest agricultural advances. Some built huge buildings that combined a number of farming operations under one roof, from feeding, sheltering, and milking the cows to pumping the manure out to fertilize the fields. Steam-driven plows, reapers, and other newly invented farm machines were housed in a variety of stone structures. The era of high farming—and the extravagant investments in new buildings and technology—came to a screeching halt at the start of the agricultural depression in the 1870s.

COUNTRY COTTAGES

Farmers provided their regular laborers with a cottage, either free or at low rent. Casual workers found their own lodging, often in shacks in open villages or market towns. Of all the country cottages, those in estate villages were usually (but not always) the largest and most well built. Very progressive landowners built model villages on their estates, bringing in architects to design solid stone or brick dwellings, each with four or five rooms and a large garden.

These comfortable cottages were the exception. Most landowners, farmers, and builders were unwilling or unable to invest the money needed to build and maintain high-quality laborers' housing. As a result, most farmworkers lived in dwellings that were little better than the slum tenements in overcrowded cities.

Two elderly women share a meager meal in a mud-walled cottage.

The English writer William Howitt described the typical laborer's cottage as a "tenement of, at most, one or two rooms. His naked walls; bare brick, stone or mud floor, as it may be; a few wooden, or rush-bottomed chairs; a deal [pine], or old oak table; a simple fire-place, with its oven beside it, or, in many parts of the kingdom, no other fire-place than the hearth; a few pots and pans—and you have his whole abode."

The "naked walls" of the cottager's home were most likely mud or clay. The roof was made of thatch—layers of dry straw, reeds, and other vegetation. Thatched roofs looked pretty, but if they were not carefully maintained, they soon decayed. The cottage floors, usually packed earth or rough stones, were cold and damp in the winter and sometimes trickled with water in the springtime.

These mud-and-thatch hovels were not only uncomfortable but overcrowded. It was not uncommon for a large family to live in a cottage with only one room for living, cooking, and sleeping. Slightly larger dwellings might have a combined living room-kitchen, a small bedroom, and a little loft reached by a wood or rope ladder, which served as a second bedroom. There was no indoor plumbing. Water was usually toted from the village well. Several families shared a single privy (outdoor toilet). The refuse from overflowing privies and pigsties occasionally seeped into the water supplies or ran down village streets, collecting into foul-smelling pools. Country dwellers were healthier overall than poor urban workers. However, the unsanitary conditions in some villages led to outbreaks of the same deadly diseases—cholera, typhoid, typhus—that were ravaging the overcrowded Victorian cities.

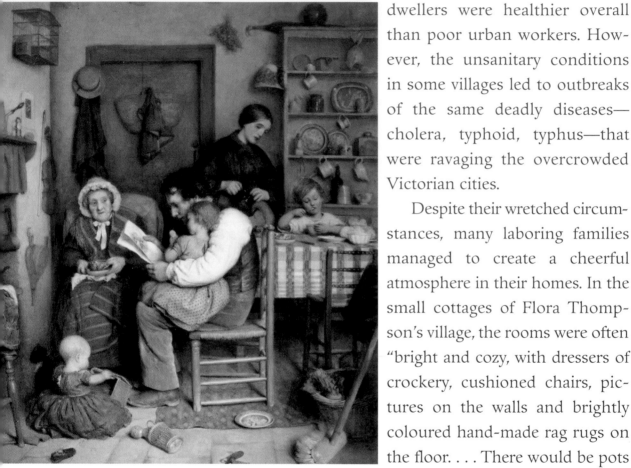

Bright table covers, crockery, and other ornaments lend a touch of cheer to a crowded country home.

Despite their wretched circumstances, many laboring families managed to create a cheerful atmosphere in their homes. In the small cottages of Flora Thompson's village, the rooms were often "bright and cozy, with dressers of crockery, cushioned chairs, pictures on the walls and brightly coloured hand-made rag rugs on the floor. . . . There would be pots of geraniums, fuchsias, and old-fashioned, sweet-smelling musk on the window-sills." Women took pride in the flowers, herbs, fruit, and vegetables that grew on their sills and in their gardens. Many writers and artists captured the variety and abundance of the cottage gardens, contributing to the Victorians' sentimental view of the "simple delights" of country living.

INSIDE A THATCHED COTTAGE

The Victorian Age was a time of rapid social changes. As the pace of life grew increasingly hectic, many people cast a wistful eye back to the old ways of life that were fast disappearing. Artists, poets, and writers nourished the longing for bygone days with romantic images of peaceful villages and cozy thatched cottages. In 1873 Francis George Heath disputed this sentimental view of country living in a book about his travels across western England. Here Heath describes the contrast between the outer charms of a little thatched cottage and the misery within its walls.

At a turn in the road, we came upon a little scene, the like of which is rarely to be met with. . . . On the right of this path there was a row of creeper-bound cottages. . . . Facing the cottages was a row of little gardens, over-shadowed by fruit-trees. . . . The walls of some of the cottages were almost hidden by the plants and shrubs which trailed upon them, and the little "nook" was shut in, on almost every side, by orchards. . . . There in very truth were the "cottage homes," situated in one of the most beautiful spots in the beautiful west of England. . . .

We caught sight of a child without shoes sitting on a doorstep. It was that of No. 1 in the row. We went up the steps, knocked at the door, and [were] asked, "Would we please to walk in?" . . . In the one miserable downstair room were grouped these ragged creatures [a laborer and his family], looking wonderingly at us. On the table stood a brown pan, filled with butcher's offal. . . . We were . . . shown up the narrow staircase. Winding round to the right, we were not long in reaching "the first floor." . . .

Words can hardly convey with sufficient effect an impression of the abject poverty which silently but eloquently told its piteous tale in that small room! A wretched, ragged-looking bed was before us. It filled up the greater part of the room. An old brown, worn, patched tester [canopy] stretched over this bed, in which the father, mother, and the two youngest children slept. Looking at the ceiling over this tester we noticed dark stains in the plaster. . . . The rain had come in upon their bed, we were told, often and often in wet weather. . . . On the floor at the foot of the bedstead there was a nondescript heap of rags, amongst which the three elder children slept. Seven human beings in this tiny, ill-lighted room!

From his top hat to his shiny patent leather shoes, this fashionable fellow is the very picture of the English country gentleman.

THREE

THE LORD
of the MANOR

Certainly there is no character in the world like that of an English
country gentleman with adequate means [and] refined tastes. . . .
What a salutary [healthful] and humanizing influence
does a man of this sort give to a remote part of a remote county.

⁓THE REVEREND BENJAMIN JOHN ARMSTRONG (1876)

THE ENGLISH COUNTRY GENTLEMAN STOOD AT THE
summit of country society. While aristocrats might spend part of
their time engrossed in national politics and the London social scene,
the gentry nearly always played a major role in day-to-day rural
affairs. Along with status and power, land brought many responsibilities. A character in a play by the popular English playwright Oscar
Wilde made a wry comment about these often-costly obligations:
"Land has ceased to be either a profit or a pleasure. It gives one position, and prevents one from keeping it up."

POWERS AND RESPONSIBILITIES

A German professor visiting an English country house in 1861 was amazed by his host's busy schedule. The squire spent "most days of the week" tending to "county or parochial [parish] business," the professor noted. Those business obligations included involvement with the "Board of Guardians, Grand Jury and Quarter Sessions, police business, inspection of prisons, workhouse, reformatory schools, parish schools, and lunatic asylum, Petty Sessions, [and] Local Board of Health."

This active squire was most likely a justice of the peace. Justices were the chief authorities of the parish, appointed to their posts by the queen. They included prominent landowners as well as leading clergymen, retired military officers, and other important men. These powerful officials judged legal cases and handed out sentences. A single justice could deal with minor offenses, such as vandalism and public drunkenness, at the Petty Sessions. More serious cases were heard when all the justices in the county met together four times a year at the Quarter Sessions. The justices' other responsibilities included regulating fairs and markets, inspecting the jails and other county institutions, organizing public works such as repairs to roads and bridges, and sitting on the Board of Guardians, which dispensed charity and supervised the workhouses where needy people received food and lodging in return for labor. A justice of the peace might spend several days a week tending to parish business, in return for little more than the esteem of his neighbors and the satisfaction of serving the community.

Only a minority of country gentlemen served as justices, but all substantial landowners had an obligation to look after their tenants and cottagers. In the Victorian view, the ideal squire was one who managed his property wisely, improving his farms and keeping the

A SQUIRE AND HIS MOTHER

While most laborers shrugged off the paternal attitude that came along with the squire's generosity, there was also resentment about the way the landowners dominated village life. Some squires were especially overbearing, telling the cottagers how to dress, what to plant in their gardens, and what church to attend. The women of the manor could be arrogant, too, dispensing unwelcome advice and criticism along with their charity. Here Flora Thompson describes a middle-aged squire and his mother who clung to their high-and-mighty ways even as the power of the gentry declined in the 1880s.

It would be almost impossible for any one born in [the twentieth] century to imagine the pride and importance of such small country gentlepeople in the 'eighties. . . . By virtue of having been born in a particular caste [class] and of living in the "big house" of the parish, they expected to reign over their poorer neighbours and to be treated by them with the deference due to royalty. . . .

A good many of the cottagers still played up to them, the women curtseying to the ground when their carriage passed and speaking in awed tones in their presence. Others, . . . having breathed the new free air of democracy, which was then beginning to percolate even into such remote places, were inclined to laugh at their pretensions. "We don't want nothin' from they," they would say, "and us shouldn't get it if us did. Let the old gal stay at home and see that her own tea-caddy's kept locked up, not come nosing round here axin' how many spoonsful we puts in ours."

[The squire's mother] knew nothing of such speeches. If she had, she would probably have thought the world—her world—was coming to an end. Which it was. In her girlhood . . . , she had been taught her duty towards the cottagers, and that included reproving [criticizing] them for their wasteful habits.

Above: A young lady pays a charitable visit to a less fortunate neighbor.

laborers' cottages in good repair. He supported the village church and school. He lowered his tenants' rents in bad times and gave generously to sick and elderly cottagers. The wise squire was careful to bestow his charity only on the truly deserving, and he never hesitated to punish laziness or dishonesty, even if that meant evicting the guilty parties from their homes. In short, he acted like a firm but loving father to his dependents.

Toward the end of the Victorian period, the traditional place of the landowner in country society began to change. Government was taking over more and more of the functions once performed by the squire: building schools, providing relief to the poor, supervising the prisons and police forces. In 1888 Parliament gave most of the gentry's remaining powers to county councils made up of elected officials. These developments did not spell the end of the landed classes. Many former justices of the peace were elected to the new councils, where they served alongside tenant farmers, small landowners, and middle-class doctors and lawyers. Many farmers and cottagers continued to admire the wealth, property, and refinement of the aristocrats and gentry. However, the old social order, in which land automatically guaranteed supremacy, was on its way out. In its place would come the very beginnings of a new age in which talented men of all classes would have a chance to earn power and privilege.

A COUNTRY HOUSE PARTY

The country gentleman's life was not all business. While he might devote many hours to his estate and local affairs, he also had an active social life. Members of the squire's family socialized with people of suitably high rank at dinners, balls, and other entertainments. The guest list to these elegant get-togethers might include neighboring squires and clergymen, along with a few "substantial" families from the neighborhood, such as a prominent banker or lawyer and his wife.

Men and women at the peak of society took part in one of the countryside's most exclusive social rituals, the house party. Only the most elite of the elite—about 1,500 aristocratic families and gentry with very large estates—were considered "in society." These wealthy people spent much of the spring and summer at their town houses in London. In the fall they retired to the country, where they engaged in a round of visits to one another's great estates.

A fashionable house party could stretch over several days or even weeks. The daily routine was similar from one manor house to another. The day began with breakfast, usually an informal meal at which guests served themselves from a table heaped with eggs, ham, bacon, fish, toast, muffins, and other substantial fare. After breakfast the ladies occupied themselves with reading, writing letters, embroidering, or strolling through the estate gardens. Meanwhile, the men headed out for some kind of sporting activity, usually shooting. Substantial landowners employed gamekeepers to raise game on their estates and protect the birds and animals from poachers. As the shooting party traipsed through the woods and fields, men and boys hired as "beaters" rustled the grass and bushes to drive out the game. One celebrated shooting party in January 1864 stretched over three days, with the hunters killing 4,045 pheasants, 3,902 rabbits, and various other creatures.

Another popular upper-class country sport was fox hunting. Foxes were regarded as pests because they preyed on game, and hunting them was considered not only great fun but also noble and manly. Gentlemen on horseback chased their quarry all over the countryside, with specially trained foxhounds leading the way. After

Well-dressed ladies
and gentlemen
mingle at a very
elegant (and very
costly) reception.

the hounds caught and killed the fox, its head, tail, and paws were taken as trophies.

The climax of a fashionable day in the country was dinner. Men changed from their sports coats and tweeds to long black frock coats for this formal event. Each gentleman escorted an elegantly gowned lady into the candlelit dining room, where an army of footmen served vast quantities of food. There might be as many as thirty dishes, including everything from soup and fish to a variety of meats, poultry, game, and vegetables to desserts of fruit, ices, and other sweets.

Entertaining on such a grand scale was expensive, but it had its rewards. Gentlemen and ladies alike enjoyed socializing and sharing the latest news and gossip. Ambitious people took the opportunity to arrange business deals, political alliances, and marriages for their children. Hosting an elegant house party was also a good way for rich industrialists and other up-and-coming middle-class men to charm their way into the top ranks of country society.

By the mid-1800s, age-old systems of farming were changing, but many farmers still sowed seed by hand.

FOUR

THE MEN of the FARMS

Only a man harrowing clods
In a slow silent walk,
With an old horse that stumbles and nods
Half asleep as they stalk.

Only thin smoke without flame
From the heaps of couch grass:
Yet this will go onward the same
Though Dynasties pass.
— THOMAS HARDY, "IN TIME OF 'THE BREAKING OF NATIONS'" (1915)

THE SQUIRES AND ARISTOCRATS OWNED THE LAND, but it was the farmers and laborers who made it productive. While nearly all farmers were tenants, the lifestyle of the gentleman farmer was very different from that of the smallholder on his few acres of land. An even wider gulf stretched between the gentleman farmer and the men who labored from sunrise to sunset in his fields.

GENTLEMEN FARMERS AND SMALLHOLDERS

The majority of Victorian farms practiced "mixed farming," producing both crops and livestock. The main crops were grains, especially wheat, oats, and barley. Cattle provided beef, hides, and milk. Sheep were raised for their wool and mutton. Most farmers also kept a few pigs and chickens. Many rotated their grain crops with clover and root vegetables such as turnips to "rest" the soil and help feed the animals.

The gentlemen farmers on large farms did not plant the crops or look after the livestock themselves. Instead, they were basically managers who organized the work of their laborers. A good-sized farm of six hundred acres might have twenty to thirty regular laborers, while the largest farms had seventy or more. A bailiff helped the farmer supervise the men, making sure they worked hard and efficiently at the most urgent tasks.

At busy times of the year, the gentleman farmer got up early, met with his bailiff to organize the day's schedule, then spent the day tending to farm business. During more quiet intervals, he might go riding or fishing, visit friends and relatives, or travel to markets and farmers' club meetings. Enterprising farmers also read the agricultural journals and attended agricultural shows to keep informed on the latest advances in farming methods and technology.

Farmers on smaller plots of land had far less leisure time. They not only supervised their laborers but often worked alongside them in the fields and farmyard. A smallholder might invest in inexpensive new farm implements, but the larger and more sophisticated machines were out of his reach.

The smallholder's simple diet consisted mainly of bread, potatoes, fish, salt pork, seasonal fruits or vegetables, and a cut of fresh meat on Sundays. Meanwhile, the gentleman farmer enjoyed the same ample meals as the squire, including dinners featuring several courses of soups, meats, fish, seafood, vegetables, pies, and puddings. The largest farmers were men of considerable influence in the local community, often serving on the boards that managed the schools and workhouses. Although they did not attend the squire's formal dinner parties and balls, they looked forward to an occasional invitation to a fox hunt or shooting party. By law, tenant farmers were forbidden to shoot game on a landowner's estate. However, a squire could "deputize" a non-landowner, temporarily granting him permission to shoot inside the private preserves.

Despite these occasional concessions, the social relations between tenants and landlords were strictly limited. "If the farming men now and then mix with the landowners in their field sports," observed the politician William Johnston, "it is upon a footing of understood inferiority, and the association exists only out of doors." Toward the end of the Victorian period, these distinctions would begin to fade. As the traditional powers and privileges of the country squires waned, gentlemen farmers often moved to fill the void. Many were elected to the new county councils. Some former tenants even bought large plots of land from their landlords, becoming important landowners themselves.

A YEAR ON THE FARM

Throughout the Victorian period, most of the work on farms was still performed by human and animal power. The farm laborers' work varied according to a number of factors, including region, climate, local traditions, and the farmer's personal inclinations. Despite these differences, nearly all English farms followed a basic seasonal calendar.

The agricultural year began with the preparation of the fields in midwinter. Horses pulled the plows that turned the soil and cut the furrows. They dragged the sharp-toothed harrows that broke up the remaining clods of earth. Winter was also the time for the birthing of lambs. Shepherds kept watch day and night, protecting the flock from predators and making sure the mothers took good care of their newborns.

The first grain was planted in late winter. The seed might be sown by hand or, increasingly, by a mechanical seed drill that dropped it into the furrows. As the crops grew, laborers hoed and yanked out an endless profusion of thistles, couch grass, and other weeds. Meanwhile, the shepherds and cowmen drove the sheep and cattle to the meadows to graze. Around the end of May, shepherds sheared the sheep's thick wool with metal blades.

Early summer was haymaking season. The farmer often hired men and women from the village to help the regular farmhands at this busy time. The workers mowed the long grass with handheld tools called scythes, gathered it into bushels, and laid it in the fields to dry. Later they stored the hay in the barn or built it into stacks, which were covered with thatched roofs to guard against the rain.

A farmer fills his barn with a bountiful crop of hay.

By late July or August, the grain was ripe. The entire neighborhood helped bring in the harvest, with the regular workers joined by roving labor gangs and village men, women, and children of all ages and occupations. On some farms teams of strong men sliced through the tall stalks with short sickles or longer scythes. By the 1870s, about one-quarter of English farms had converted to mechan-

ical reapers with long, revolving arms. Workers followed behind the harvest teams, gathering up the fallen sheaves, binding them, and setting them up in "stooks"—groups of sheaves standing up together. Once the grain dried, it was loaded onto wagons and brought to the farmyard. There it was put up in stacks or "ricks," which were covered with cloth or thatch. Every one of these tasks had to be performed quickly. If the late summer rains came before the harvest was completed, if the grain lay on the ground or the ricks stood uncovered, half of the farm's yearly income could be lost.

After the grain was harvested, it was bound into sheaves and set up to dry.

After the last harvest wagon came in, the farmer allowed the village women to go "gleaning," or scouring the fields for stray grain, which they took home to help feed their families and livestock. The farmer also treated all his workers to a lively feast called "harvest home." That festive celebration marked the end of the main growing season. For the regular laborers, however, there was still much work to be done. There were apples to gather and potatoes, turnips, and other root crops to dig up. There were fields to fertilize, beans and other winter crops to sow, and sheep and cattle to drive to market.

Over the long winter months, the pace of work slowed. Laborers trimmed the hedges, mended the fences, cleared ditches, and cared for the livestock. They threshed the harvested grain for market, separating the edible grain from the chaff. In the early Victorian period,

BREAD AND ONIONS

Many cottagers lived on little more than bread and potatoes. A laborer who earned slightly higher wages might be able to afford cheese, eggs, and perhaps a small cut of mutton or other meat for Sunday dinner. Fortunate cottagers kept a pig, which provided them with pork, bacon, sausages, and other occasional treats. Fruits and vegetables grown in the cottage garden might round out the menu, although these were often sold to supplement the family's income. During a 1901 tour of rural England, the agricultural reformer Rider Haggard met one impoverished farmworker who described a lifetime of bread and onions. As the man noted, the late nineteenth century brought slow but steady improvements to the diet of cottage families.

I saw an old labourer named John Lapwood, whose life experience, which I verified by inquiry, is worth preserving. . . . He stated that for months at a time he had existed upon nothing but a diet of bread and onions, washed down, when he was lucky, with a little small-beer [weak beer]. These onions he ate until they took the skin off the roof of his mouth, blistering it to whiteness. . . . They had no tea, but his wife imitated the appearance of that beverage by soaking a burnt crust of bread in boiling water. On this diet he became so feeble that the reek of the muck which it was his duty to turn, made him sick and faint; and often, he said, he would walk home at night from the patch of ground where he grew the onions and some other vegetables, with swimming head and uncertain feet. I asked if his children, of whom there were eight, lived on onions also. He answered no; they had generally a little cheese and butter in the house, but he could not put it into his own stomach when they were hungry and cried for food. "Things is better now" he added.

Above: Laborers turn the hard soil on a frosty late-winter morning.

near large towns and cities, where there were fewer farmworkers and more job opportunities.

To make ends meet, a farm laborer might take on additional jobs after his regular workday ended. His wife and children often worked, too. From time to time, farmers provided their laborers with potatoes, flour, milk, beer, or cider, either as part of their pay or as bonuses. Despite these extras, a setback such as a long illness, injury, or layoff could bring a laboring family close to starvation.

In the last few decades of the nineteenth century, farmworkers' wages began to rise. The increase was partly due to the labor shortages that resulted as workers left the countryside. Newly organized agricultural unions also won pay raises and greater political rights for rural workers. By the end of the century, most rural laborers were still poor, but their lives were slowly improving.

COUNTRY CRAFTSMEN

While the great majority of men living in the Victorian countryside worked in agriculture, a significant number were involved in crafts and trades. These skilled workers played an important role in country life. The goods and services they provided were vital to the smooth running of the farms and the community in general.

The most important rural craftsman was the blacksmith. He performed a wide range of tasks: shoeing horses, repairing plows, and sharpening harrows for the farmer; making hammers, chisels, and other tools for fellow craftsmen; repairing leaky cooking pots for local housewives. The blacksmith's workshop was often a lively place, where men swapped news and stories in their idle moments, as young boys gazed in fascination at the blazing forge fire. To one impressionable boy, the "reek of the burning hoof, as the hot shoe was pressed on it, the smith's language when the horse would not

The village black-smith could perform nearly any job involving metal. This smith is shoeing a horse.

'side still', the clanging anvil and flying sparks, all conjured up a sort of Sunday School picture of hell with the smith himself as a kindly sort of devil."

Other craftsmen commonly found in even a small village included the shoemaker, carpenter, and wheelwright (who made and repaired wooden wheels, tools, carts, and wagons). Larger villages and market towns were home to specialists in a wider variety of crafts and trades. Among these were bakers, brewers, bricklayers, carriers (who toted goods and passengers in their horse-drawn carts), coopers (who made wooden tubs and barrels), farriers (who doctored horses), glaziers (who worked with glass), masons (who cut and carved building stones), millers (who ground grain), saddle and harness makers, tailors, and thatchers (who covered roofs and haystacks with thatch).

In the last few decades of the nineteenth century, the declining rural population and the rising flood of inexpensive factory-made products chipped away at the country craftsman's business. Mass-produced plows, carts, ladders, clothing, and shoes gradually replaced the handcrafted work of blacksmiths, wheelwrights, carpenters, tailors, and shoemakers. Water- and wind-driven mills stopped turning as farmers sent their grain to the steam-powered mills of big flour companies.

Some country tradesmen hung on to their old businesses, repairing the increasingly old-fashioned tools that were still used on many farms well into the early twentieth century. Some adapted to the changing times. A blacksmith might become a machinist, specializing in the maintenance of farm machinery. A miller might install his own steam engine. Many other craftsmen left the countryside for jobs in the towns and cities or emigrated to countries where their skills were still in demand. A government commission investigating rural working conditions in the early 1900s summed up the slow disappearance of village crafts: "There was hardly any money to be made . . . , and all the young men went to the factories and the boys ceased to learn the trades."

Women gather up leftover grain after the harvest, binding it into miniature sheaves to carry home to their families.

G. CLAUSEN

FIVE

THE WOMEN *of the* COUNTRYSIDE

To the women, home was home in a special sense. . . .
There they washed and cooked and cleaned and mended
for their teeming families; there they enjoyed their precious
half-hour's peace with a cup of tea before the fire in the afternoon;
there they bore their troubles as best they could
and cherished their few joys.

⟶ FLORA THOMPSON, *LARK RISE TO CANDLEFORD*

WHILE THE WIFE OF A SQUIRE OR ARISTOCRAT LIVED A life of ease, the majority of rural women worked even harder than the men. The women of the farms and villages were responsible for nearly all the work done in the home. Many also worked on the farm or at paying jobs. "The agricultural labourer's wife, indeed, has a harder lot than her husband," observed the English writer Richard Jefferies. "His toil is for the most part over when he leaves the field, but the woman's is never finished."

Upper-class Victorian ladies had the time, money, and education to pursue pleasurable pursuits such as reading.

THE SQUIRE'S LADY AND THE FARMER'S WIFE

Upper-class Victorian women were not expected to work. They had servants to tend to the household chores, help them dress, fix their hair, and watch over their children. That left country gentlewomen with lots of free time. They might while away the hours reading books or indulging in "feminine" pursuits such as needlework, sketching, painting with watercolors, and playing the harp or piano. When the weather was fine, they took long walks and went horseback riding. Well-to-do women also spent a good deal of time visiting back and forth with friends and relatives.

Planning a dinner or house party was the closest some elegant ladies ever came to real work. Others devoted many hours to charitable activities. The squire's wife might stop by the village school to encourage the students and teachers. She often visited sick and elderly villagers, bringing gifts of food, clothing, and homemade remedies. At Christmastime she distributed coal and blankets to needy families.

The women of the farms led far more active lives than even the busiest lady of the manor. On all but the largest holdings, the farmer's wife might feed the chickens, tend to chores in the dairy, and lend a hand whenever and wherever else she was needed. She was also responsible for the cooking, cleaning, washing, and other household chores.

Most farmwives had one or more servants to help them with their many time-consuming tasks. In the days before electric appliances, simply washing the laundry was a wearisome job that could take two women four or five days. First the women fetched water from the well to soak the soiled linens. The next day they heated more water in large copper washtubs. They scrubbed the laundry with soap, rinsed and wrung it out several times, and hung it to dry. Dyed fabrics, wool, and other special items had to be washed separately, in different water temperatures, with various additives to protect them. After the laundry was dry, it had to be starched, aired out, and ironed. By the time the last sheet was folded and put away, it was nearly time to start the process all over again.

A Victorian household manual described washing the laundry as "very hard work; more young women break down their strength with washing than with any other toil."

THE WOMEN OF THE VILLAGE

In the early Victorian period, most laboring families could not afford the basic necessities of life without the extra income earned by wives and children. Women who worked on farms were usually casual laborers, hired on at busy times such as haymaking and the harvest. More than half of the workers in roving agricultural labor gangs were young girls and women.

Other women worked on the land full-time. These hardy female laborers put their hands to nearly all the tasks performed by men, except plowing and ditch digging. When the gentleman lawyer Arthur Munby toured the northern English countryside in 1862, he met "a gang of twelve stout women and girls, all in white smocks and rustic bonnets and kerchiefs, picking potatoes." The women were "stooping or kneeling on the ground, and digging up the potatoes with their hands." They would each earn a shilling for a workday that stretched from seven or eight in the morning to dusk. One young woman told Munby that she worked that way year-round, "at hay and harvest, at pea picking in June, at osier [twig]-peeling in May, at tater gathering in October, and then at turnip pulling, and so on."

Along with farmwork, there were a variety of other ways for countrywomen to add to the family's income. The wife of a laborer, craftsman, or small farmer might take in washing, ironing, or sewing. Some women practiced traditional skills such as nursing the sick or delivering babies. Many more worked in "cottage industries." Before the Industrial Revolution, rural women had traditionally earned extra money by spinning thread and weaving cloth in their cottages. By the time Victoria became queen, the textile factories had put an end to that business. However, a number of other traditional crafts lingered on for several decades.

Some of the most widely practiced cottage industries were lace making, glove making, button making, and straw plaiting (braiding straw for hats). Mothers and daughters might ply their trade at home, or several women might work together in one of their cottages. One woman took charge of bringing the finished products to a nearby town for sale and returning with new supplies of raw materials.

As factory production expanded, the cottage industries died out. In 1851 there were more than 10,000 female lace makers in the county of Buckinghamshire and a similar number of straw plaiters in Bedfordshire. Fifty years later, Buckinghamshire had 789 lace makers, and only 485 plaiters were left in Bedfordshire.

The closing decades of the nineteenth century also saw a sharp drop in the number of female farm laborers, from nearly 200,000 in

1851 to about 12,000 in 1901. The decline was due partly to the continuing migration of country folk to towns and cities and partly to the loss of jobs to farm machinery. It also reflected the gradual rise in male laborers' wages. As men began to earn more money, women were expected to take their "proper" place in the home and devote themselves to caring for their husbands and children.

AROUND THE HEARTH FIRE

Raising a family in a small, run-down cottage was no easy task. "Everything had to be done practically in one room," recalled George Sturt, who grew up in a village in southern England. "The preparation and serving of meals, the airing of clothes and the ironing of them, the washing of the children, the mending and making—how could a woman do any of it with comfort in the cramped apartment?"

The typical laborer's cottage had no running water. Some families set a barrel against an outside wall to collect rainwater, which could be used for bathing, washing the laundry, and watering the garden.

Three generations work and play in one room of a small country cottage.

Water for drinking and cooking was toted in buckets from the village pump or well. As a child, Flora Thompson watched the women of her village trudge home with the heavy buckets "suspended from their shoulders by a yoke. Those were weary journeys . . . , and many were the rests and endless was the gossip, as they stood at corners in their big white aprons and crossover shawls." When summer droughts dried up the village wells, the women had to fetch water from a pump at a farmhouse half a mile away.

During the daytime, women did their household chores by the dim light filtering through the cottage windows. At night, light was provided by the hearth fire and, in early Victorian times, by rushlights— simple candles made by peeling rushes and soaking them in mutton grease. In the 1850s cottage interiors grew brighter with the use of lamps that burned an inexpensive new oil-based fuel called paraffin.

Women traditionally cooked the family's meals in a pot hanging over the fire. Bread might be baked in a brick oven set into the wall beside the hearth or in a closed container called a "pot oven," which was placed in the fire and covered with smoldering embers. By the 1880s, many cottages had coal-burning cast-iron ranges.

No matter how small or cramped, a cottage was home to the people who lived there. In the evenings families gathered around the hearth for warmth, comfort, and companionship. "After working in the pure cold air of the fields all day," wrote Flora Thompson,

> the men found it comforting to be met by, and wrapped round in, an atmosphere of chimney-smoke and bacon and cabbage-cooking; to sink into "feyther's [father's] chair" by the hearth, draw off heavy, mud-caked boots, take the latest baby on their knee and sip strong, sweet tea while "our Mum" dished up the tea-supper.

"A PUDDING MADE OF SMALL BIRDS"

Cooking was a challenge for a village woman with limited resources. In 1852 Charles Elmé Francatelli, a former chef to Queen Victoria, published a cookbook intended to show the poor cottager how to "prepare and cook your daily food, so as to obtain from it the greatest amount of nourishment at the least possible expense." Here are Francatelli's instructions for preparing "A Pudding Made of Small Birds." While few modern-day diners may smack their lips over this recipe, accounts from the Victorian countryside confirm that laboring families sometimes ate stews, pies, puddings, and dumplings made from small birds such as sparrows. As one man explained, "A lot o' people never tasted meat, and that was better than no meat at all."

Industrious and intelligent boys who live in the country, are mostly well up in the cunning art of catching small birds at odd times during the winter months. So, my young friends, when you have been so fortunate as to succeed in making a good catch of a couple of dozen of birds, you must first pluck them free from feathers, cut off their heads and claws, and pick out their gizzards from their sides with the point of a small knife, and then hand the birds over to your mother, who, by following these instructions, will prepare a famous pudding for your dinner or supper. First, fry the birds whole with a little butter, shalot [shallot], parsley, thyme, and winter savory, all chopped small, pepper and salt to season; and when the birds are half done, shake in a small handful of flour, add rather better than a gill [five ounces] of water, stir the whole on the fire while boiling for ten minutes, and when the stew of birds is nearly [cooked], pour it all into a good-sized pudding basin, which has been ready-lined with either a suet and flour crust, or else a dripping-crust, cover the pudding in with a piece of the paste, and either bake or boil it for about an hour and-a-half.

Above: A woman cooks on a brick oven beside an open hearth.

A little girl plays a toy drum, in a photograph taken around 1865.

SIX

COUNTRY LADS
and LASSES

Eight appears to be the ordinary age at which children
of both sexes join the common [agricultural labor] gang,
although seven is not unusual. . . . One little girl
only four years old was carried by her father to the fields,
and put to work under a gangmaster.

⁓ "AGRICULTURAL GANGS," *QUARTERLY REVIEW*, 1867

THE LIVES OF COUNTRY BOYS AND GIRLS WERE SHAPED
by their families' social class and income. The children of squires
and aristocrats grew up amid wealth and plenty but often spent more
time with the household staff than with their parents. Village children
were poorly fed, clothed, and housed. They were put to work young,
helping their mothers around the house and toiling outside the
home for wages. Despite these hardships, people raised in poor
laboring families often looked back on childhood as a time of
warmth, closeness, and shared challenges.

AN UPPER-CLASS UPBRINGING

The children of upper-class Victorian families spent most of their time in the nursery and schoolroom. They were raised by a nanny or nursemaids, and most of their early education was provided by governesses and tutors. Fanny Cowper, who grew up on a large country estate in southern England, later spoke of her lonely childhood. While their aristocratic parents traveled, Fanny and the other Cowper children were left in the care of a strict nanny and an unkind governess. The nanny, Mrs. Hawk, punished the smallest misbehavior by calling for the "Jalap pot," which contained a "nauseous mixture" that caused vomiting and diarrhea. The governess, Miss Tomkinson, was so unkind that Fanny "once gave her a catseye ring I had to propitiate [pacify] her."

Well-born Victorian girls were expected to pass their time with quiet activities such as drawing, needlework, and reading.

Of course, the life of a well-to-do Victorian child was not always gloomy. Girls and boys were well dressed (although their clothes were often uncomfortably fussy) and well fed (on food that was bland but "wholesome"). They had plenty of playthings, including dolls, rocking horses, model castles, toy soldiers, and all sorts of games and puzzles. When their parents were home, they often spent at least part of each day with their mother. Lady Cowper took her children along to church and on charitable visits to needy cottagers.

The future course of the Cowper children's lives, like those of other upper-class boys and girls, was largely set at birth. By law and tradition, estates were nearly always passed down from a father to his firstborn son. Most great estates were "entailed," or tied up by a legal agreement that gave the heir the income from the land but not the right to sell it. These restrictions ensured that a landed family's property would pass down intact from generation to generation. The oldest son could count on living off the income from the property he would inherit. Younger sons looked for wealthy wives or trained for careers in the military, law, or clergy.

Girls had fewer options than their brothers. In most cases they could expect to inherit little more than a small support settlement. Respectable women did not work, so they could not plan for careers. That meant that a well-born Victorian girl had to marry, and marry well, in order to maintain a lifestyle befitting a lady. Her education revolved mainly around accomplishments designed to display her good breeding and attract a husband: fine needlework, drawing, painting, speaking French or German, playing the piano.

The daughters of aristocrats and important country squires "came out" at around age eighteen. Their passage into fashionable society was marked by a formal ceremony at court, where nervous "debutantes" dressed in long white gowns curtseyed and kissed the queen's hand. Once a girl entered society, her mother eagerly scouted out a suitable match, preferably to the oldest son of a long-established family. The negotiations preceding the marriage were about as romantic as a business merger. Lawyers for both sides hammered out a settlement specifying the bride's dowry (the amount of money she would bring to the marriage), the allowance her husband would give her while he lived, and how much he would leave to support her and any young children when he died. After the settlement was signed, the couple was married in an elaborate church ceremony. Many Victorian brides wore white wedding gowns, a custom that was inspired by Queen Victoria's wedding in 1840 and continues to the present day.

THE YOUNGEST WORKERS

There were no lonely days in the nursery for village lads and lasses. With the average-sized family of eight squeezed into a small one- or two-room cottage, there were no lonely days for *anyone*. Children played outdoors, at games requiring little more than imagination: hide and seek, blind man's bluff, "Here we go round the mulberry bush." A plank of wood laid over a log became a seesaw and, as one youngster recalled, "a little stool made a capital [excellent] make-believe engine for the small boy."

While they were still very young, village children began to help their mother, fetching water, gathering firewood, and feeding the family pig. Girls who were "scarcely more than infants themselves" often took care of their younger brothers and sisters, observed William Howitt. "The little creatures go lugging about great fat babies that really seem as heavy as themselves."

Children also worked outside the home. Boys and girls as young as seven or eight could earn a few pennies weeding farm fields or scaring birds away from the crops. As they grew older, they might help drive the farm carts, milk the cows, or herd the sheep and goats. In the early Victorian period, children also worked in agricultural labor gangs. A government commission found that child laborers sometimes walked several miles to and from work, beginning their day before sunrise and returning home after dark. The youngsters were expected to work as long and hard as grown-up laborers at exhausting tasks: cutting and hauling hay, clearing away stones, digging up turnips and potatoes. Reports of these appalling conditions eventually caused a public outcry. In 1867 Parliament passed a law forbidding the employment of children under age eight in agricultural gangs. While the regulations gradually did away with some of the worst abuses in gang labor, many young children continued to work hard as casual laborers.

Other children worked in cottage industries. Some learned their craft from their mother, while others were sent to special craft

Child laborers trudge home after a long, hard day of work in farm fields.

A LIFE IN SERVICE

When a cottager's daughter was between ten and fifteen years old, her family usually tried to find her a place "in service." Most girls started out as a maid-of-all-work in the home of a local farmer or tradesman. After they had some experience, they could look for a better position in a big country house or nearby town or city.

The diaries of Florence Stowe, a girl from a village in the county of Warwickshire, give us an idea of the demanding life of a Victorian farm servant. Florence's daily chores included cleaning the farmhouse, preparing meals, and helping in the dairy. Each morning before breakfast, she had to strain and heat the milk that was fed to the calves. After the cowman milked the cows, she would

clean all the Milk Pans and separator and strainer and milk buckets, swill [wash out] the dairy. . . . I would then get all veg[etables] and sundries [other items] for cooking, dinner was served at 12.30. Each day [also] brought its own particular job, mostly done in the afternoons. One was set aside for churning and making the butter, a 2-hour work and about 30 to 40 lb. to pot up, weigh, mark ready for market. . . . Another afternoon was taken up to clean all Brass, Copper, Silver and Meat Dish covers and brass kettles.

Florence also had "all the wood and coal to get in for all fires." She helped out at busy times such as haymaking, harvesting, and threshing. After a long day of work, she might trudge upstairs around 10 p.m. and fall into bed exhausted.

Above: Domestic servants worked hard, but most could count on plenty of food and a clean, comfortable home.

schools, usually beginning at around age five or six. These schools were more like workshops than educational institutions. A woman skilled in straw plaiting or lace making might give lessons and supervise young workers in her cottage. As many as twenty or thirty students were crammed into one small, stuffy room lit by candles or rushlights. The younger children might work four to eight hours a day, the older ones twelve hours or longer.

In 1867 Parliament made cottage industries subject to the same laws that restricted child labor in factories. These regulations were almost impossible to enforce, however, in rural districts where hard-pressed families depended on their children's earnings. Young girls and boys would continue to spend long hours laboring over lace pillows, straw plait, and other crafts until the decline of the cottage industries toward the end of the century.

MOVING UP, MOVING OUT

For much of the nineteenth century, the education of country children was a hit-or-miss affair. The children of squires and aristocrats were taught by tutors and governesses, after which many went on to prestigious boarding schools. The farmer's children also might go to boarding schools (although not the same expensive institutions that educated the squire's sons). Meanwhile, it was a matter of chance whether a laborer's child received even a basic education. In the early Victorian period, many villages had no school at all. Some had elementary schools supported with funds donated by a generous landowner or raised by the local clergyman. Charitable and religious groups also operated a number of elementary schools, often with aid from the national government. In addition, some older women and men gave lessons in their homes, although these "dame schools" were often little more than babysitting services.

The Elementary Education Act of 1870 required the establishment of elementary schools throughout England and Wales. Where no schools existed, newly formed school boards were responsible for building and maintaining them. These reforms were a big step in the right direction, but it would take several decades before they resulted in real advances in rural education. Conditions in country schools made it hard for students to learn. Children of all ages were crowded into one or two rooms, where they endured dull lessons focusing mainly on the "three Rs": reading, (w)riting, and (a)rithmetic. They spent most of their time practicing their penmanship and memorizing long lists of facts.

Another major problem at rural schools was poor attendance. Parliament passed laws requiring all children to attend school until age ten (later raised to fourteen), but the regulations were widely ignored. Some laborers with little education themselves could not see the value of it for their children. Even those who appreciated the importance of schooling often could not spare their children's earnings or afford to pay the school fees (education did not become free until 1891). Parents frequently took their sons and daughters out of school to work on farms or in cottage industries. Some children worked before and after school hours and on weekends. These young workers often came to the classroom too tired and hungry to concentrate on their lessons.

As soon as they were old enough to earn a living, many young country people left school completely. Girls might go into service. Boys might work on the land or enlist in the army. The son of a blacksmith, carpenter, or other craftsman often followed his father in the family trade.

Young country men and women usually married sometime in their twenties. They wore their Sunday-best clothes to the simple church ceremony. The newlyweds might start out living with one of their families, or they might lodge in their own small cottage and begin raising their own children.

Meanwhile, increasing numbers of young men and women were leaving the countryside to seek their fortunes in the towns and cities. "When the children got a little education," recalled one former schoolmaster,

> they began to look down on their parents' condition, and I have often heard boys say: "I'll never be a farmer's drudge if I can help it." . . . Thus the bone and sinew of our villages go away leaving the old and infirm to do the work, and every year men get scarcer.

The Little-One's Own

Coloured Picture Paper

Edited by Mrs Eliz.th Day

TOBY'S AUDIENCE

Come along and let us go to look at Punch and Judy, it is so funny and lots of people are enjoying it already. — Poor TOBY sits there so prettily, asking you as well as he can to come and look at him, dressed in his large white ruffle. — Mr. Punch is telling him to sit up and be a good doggie, and to do what he is told to do, as all good little boys and girls ought also to do.

Above: **Grown-ups and children enjoy a Punch and Judy show—a popular puppet show performed by traveling players in England from the seventeenth century through today.**

SEVEN

"ALL MIRTH and JOLLITY"

When young or progressive inhabitants . . .
complained of the dullness of village life,
the more staid would say, "It may be dull in some villages;
but not here. Why, there's always something going on!"
～FLORA THOMPSON, *LARK RISE TO CANDLEFORD*

FOR THE MEN, WOMEN, AND CHILDREN OF THE VICTO-rian village, life was often a wearisome round of work, sleep, and meager meals. Social gatherings offered a welcome break from this monotonous routine. Families found most of their amusements within the village itself, enjoying singing, dancing, games, and laughter at the local church, school, inn, or public house. Market days and country fairs offered a rare chance to experience the excitement of a wider world.

THE "SIMPLE LIFE"

The center of social life in most villages was the public house, or "pub." Here small farmers and laborers passed many an evening sipping beer, singing songs, reading newspapers, and discussing local events. The men also played a variety of indoor games, including dice, dominoes, darts, and a tabletop bowling game called skittles. To the "man who labours all day in wet and storm," wrote Richard Jefferies, the pub offered "heat and light [and] amusement." It served the same purpose as the gentleman's "reading-room, his club, and his assembly rooms."

Village life also offered amusements for the entire family. There were church socials, with games and refreshments. At the local schoolhouse, cottagers attended "penny readings," paying a penny apiece to listen to speakers read aloud from popular authors such as Charles Dickens. Many parishes held an annual flower show, awarding prizes for the finest flowers, fruits, and vegetables grown in the cottage gardens. During the winter, community parties might be held in a barn lit with lamps and candles. One elderly cottager remembered enjoying all the "good things to eat" at these gatherings, followed by "a sing-song, and the country dancing."

A number of country festivities were tied to the farming calendar. Plow Monday in early January marked the first plowing of the new year. In this age-old celebration, costumed laborers paraded through the village streets, dragging a plow decked out in scarves and ribbons. At various times in the growing season, some farmers hosted special feasts for their workers. "'Twere all mirth and jollity," recalled one elderly farmworker.

> First of all there was the sower's feast,—that would be about the end of April; then came the sheep-shearer's feast,—

Villagers make merry on May Day, an ancient holiday that was still being celebrated in Victorian times.

there'd be about fifteen of us as would sit down after sheep-shearing, and we'd be singing best part of the night, and plenty to eat and drink; next came the feast for the reapers, when the corn was cut about August; and, last of all, the harvest home in September.

A few weeks after harvest home, the people of the village held their own harvest festival. Boys and girls who were working in town or on outlying farms came home for this special occasion. In larger villages the streets were lined with booths offering oranges, sausages, gingerbread, cakes, and other treats. There might be shooting galleries and a merry-go-round powered by a hand-turned crank, a pony, or, in later years, by steam. Money saved from the extra harvest pay went toward the family's dinner. "Nearly every family managed to have a joint of beef and a Yorkshire pudding," recalled Flora Thompson. "The men wore their best suits, complete with collar and tie, and the women brought out their treasured finery and wore it, for, even if no relatives from a distance were expected, some one might be 'popping in.'"

Victorian workers got time off for only a handful of religious holidays. The most important of these was Christmas. On this festive occasion, large farmers and landowners gave gifts of food, clothing, and coal to their laborers. From time to time, villages also took part in national celebrations. While the people of London celebrated Queen Victoria's Golden and Diamond Jubilees with lavish processions and fireworks, country folk enjoyed their own smaller parades, feasts, and games.

MARKETS AND FAIRS

Even the smallest village was within reach of a town. Most towns had a regular market day. On the appointed day, the roads and footpaths leading into town were crowded with country people. Farm families perched atop carts and wagons loaded with produce, poultry, eggs, cheese, butter, and honey. Cowmen drove their cattle, shepherds

Crowded with shoppers and country people from miles around, the weekly town market was a lively scene.

their sheep. Village men and women carried baskets of herbs and vegetables from their gardens. Boys and girls toted their own baskets filled with captured sparrows or bunches of flowers. All these people pushed and jostled their way to the open marketplace, where they haggled over prices with the traders and householders who came to inspect their merchandise. Once they had sold their goods, country folk often spent part of the money in the town shops, buying items such as crockery, tea, sugar, hats, shoes, fabrics, and newspapers.

Country fairs were similar to the weekly markets, only on a much larger scale. Fairs were usually annual events, held on a set day in the spring or fall. Thousands of villagers came from miles around, traveling in carts and wagons, on horseback, and by foot. Some hoped to sell a season's worth of crops, livestock, or handcrafted wares. Some were seeking jobs. At yearly hiring fairs, workers looking for new jobs carried a sign of their trade: a mop for a servant girl, a scythe for a farmhand, a crook for a shepherd. When a farmer and worker reached an agreement, the employer gave his new hire a small sum of money to seal the deal.

After the day's business was concluded, it was time for fun. Fairs offered all kinds of entertainment: magic acts, puppet shows, dancing bears, mechanical rides, boxing and wrestling matches, sideshows with oddities such as a "strong man" or two-headed calf. Merchants at booths and stalls sold a variety of snacks, from meat-filled pastries to hot potatoes to gingerbread.

By the late nineteenth century, the great regional fairs were declining. With the railway network carrying factory-made goods to the countryside and rural products to towns and cities, country folk no longer needed the fairs for buying and selling. Some fairs died out completely, while others became less a place to do business than a purely entertaining event. The railroads also affected the weekly markets, with some larger towns growing in importance and smaller markets fading away.

These changes in country amusements were just another sign of the times. Many forces were transforming the Victorian countryside: the shrinking rural population, the increasing use of farm machinery, the decline of country crafts and cottage industries, the passing away of the old social order, the intrusion of town culture into village life. Some people looked back wistfully on the "good old days." Many more looked forward to a future in which laboring families could enjoy higher wages, better living conditions, and a better education for their children.

Meanwhile, in a number of small, remote villages, the old ways lingered on into the early decades of the twentieth century. Those who "stayed at home and waited for change to come to them," said Flora Thompson,

> better educated, a little more democratic, a little more pros-perous than their parents had been, but still the same unpre-tentious, warm-hearted people, with just enough malice to give point to their wit and a growing sense of injustice which was making them begin to inquire when their turn would come to enjoy a fair share of the fruits of the earth they tilled.

GLOSSARY

aristocrats The most privileged members of the upper class, who inherited prestigious titles and large estates.

casual laborers Farmworkers who were hired by the job, or "piece," and worked for wages.

chaff The inedible parts of harvested grain, separated from the husks and stalks during threshing. *Chaff* can also mean chopped hay used as horse feed.

couch grass A type of fast-spreading grass that can be a troublesome weed.

crop rotation A farming practice in which different crops are planted in different years to improve the fertility of the soil.

gentry Members of the upper class who ranked below the aristocrats and inherited land but not titles.

harrow A farm tool with spikes or sharp disks, used to break up the soil; *harrowing* means to cultivate the soil with a harrow.

Industrial Revolution The historical period marking the introduction of power-driven machinery and the social changes that resulted. The Industrial Revolution began in England in the mid- to late 1700s.

offal The waste parts cut away when an animal is butchered.

osier A type of willow tree or shrub, whose twigs are used in making baskets.

paraffin A fuel derived from petroleum, which was first produced commercially in the 1850s.

parish The basic unit of local government in Victorian England. In the 1830s Great Britain was divided into some 15,000 parishes, ranging in size from a few clusters of country cottages to large city neighborhoods.

Parliament The national legislature of Great Britain.

regular laborers Farmworkers who were hired by the year; also called "day laborers." In addition to their wages, regular laborers usually received a cottage free or at low rent, as well as occasional gifts of coal, food, and beer or cider.

rush A marsh plant that may be used for making woven mats and chair seats or a kind of candle.

scythe (sīth) A cutting tool with a long handle and long, curving blade.

squire A term of courtesy commonly used for a man of the gentry class whose family had lived in a country community for many generations.

tenant farmers Farmers who work land that is owned by someone else, paying rent with cash and sometimes a portion of their produce.

thatch A roofing material made from woven straw or reeds.

Yorkshire pudding A puffy pastry made from a batter of eggs, milk, and flour.

FOR FURTHER READING

Ashby, Ruth. *Victorian England.* New York: Marshall Cavendish, 2003.

Chrisp, Peter. *A History of Fashion and Clothing: The Victorian Age.* New York: Facts on File, 2005.

Damon, Duane C. *Life in Victorian England.* New York: Thomson Gale, 2006.

Ferguson, Sheila. *Growing Up in Victorian Britain.* London: B. T. Batsford, 1984.

Mitchell, Sally. *Daily Life in Victorian England.* Westport, CT: Greenwood Press, 1996.

Price-Groff, Claire. *Queen Victoria and Nineteenth-Century England.* New York: Marshall Cavendish, 2003.

Swisher, Clarice. *Victorian England.* San Diego, CA: Lucent Books, 2001.

———. *Women of Victorian England.* San Diego, CA: Lucent Books, 2005.

ONLINE INFORMATION

Agricultural Revolution in England 1500-1850. Professor Mark Overton, British Broadcasting Corporation, 2005.
www.bbc.co.uk/history/british/empire_seapower/agricultural_revolution_01.shtml

Children in Victorian Britain. British Broadcasting Corporation, 2010.
www.bbc.co.uk/schools/primaryhistory/victorian_britain/

History in Focus: The Victorian Era. Institute of Historical Research, 2001.
www.history.ac.uk/ihr/Focus/Victorians/

Life in Victorian England. Copyright 1999-2010 Excelsior Information Systems.
www.aboutbritain.com/articles/life-in-victorian-england.asp

Time Traveller's Guide to Victorian Britain. Channel 4 Television, London, 2004.
www.channel4.com/history/microsites/H/history/guide19/index.html

Victorian Farm. British Broadcasting Corporation, 2009.
www.bbc.co.uk/programmes/b00gn2bl

Who Were the Victorians? Mandy Barrow, Woodlands Junior School, Tonbridge, Kent, England, 2008.
www.woodlands-junior.kent.sch.uk/Homework/victorians.html

SELECTED BIBLIOGRAPHY

Andrews, Malcolm. *Dickens on England and the English.* New York: Barnes and Noble Books, 1979.

Arnstein, Walter L. *Britain Yesterday and Today: 1830 to the Present.* 8th ed. Boston: Houghton Mifflin, 2001.

Avery, Gillian. *Victorian People in Life and in Literature.* New York: Holt, Rinehart, and Winston, 1970.

Broomfield, Andrea. *Food and Cooking in Victorian England: A History*. Westport, CT: Praeger, 2007.

Horn, Pamela. *Labouring Life in the Victorian Countryside*. Abingdon, Oxon, England: Alan Sutton, 1995.

Lasdun, Susan. *Victorians at Home*. New York: Viking, 1981.

Mingay, G. E. *Rural Life in Victorian England*. Stroud, Gloucestershire, England: Sutton Publishing, 1998.

Pike, E. Royston. *"Golden Times": Human Documents of the Victorian Age*. New York: Frederick A. Praeger, 1967.

Pool, Daniel. *What Jane Austen Ate and Charles Dickens Knew*. New York: Simon and Schuster, 1993.

Souden, David. *The Victorian Village*. London: Collins and Brown, 1991.

Sykes, Christopher Simon. *The Golden Age of the Country House*. New York: Mayflower Books, 1980.

Thompson, Flora. *Lark Rise to Candleford*. London: Oxford University Press, 1965 (first published in 3 vols., 1939-1943).

Ward, Sadie. *Seasons of Change: Rural Life in Victorian and Edwardian England*. London: George Allen and Unwin, 1982.

Wild, Martin Trevor. *Village England: A Social History of the Countryside*. London: I. B. Taurus, 2004.

Wohl, Anthony S. *Endangered Lives: Public Health in Victorian Britain*. Cambridge, MA: Harvard University Press, 1983.

SOURCES FOR QUOTATIONS

ABOUT VICTORIAN ENGLAND

p. 6 "Since it has pleased": Queen Victoria, *Queen Victoria in Her Letters and Journals*, edited by Christopher Hibbert (New York: Viking, 1985), p. 23.

p. 7 "an age of transition": Sir Henry Holland, "The Progress and Spirit of Physical Science," *Edinburgh Review*, July 1858; quoted at www.archive.org/stream/essaysonscientif00hollrich/ essaysonscientif00hollrich_djvu.txt

CHAPTER 1: A CHANGING WORLD

p. 9 "It is part": Richard Jefferies, *Hodge and His Masters*, vol. 1 (London: Smith, Elder and Co., 1880), pp. 217, 218.

p. 13 "The squire": Joseph Arch, *Joseph Arch: The Story of His Life, Told by Himself*, edited by the Countess of Warwick (London: Hutchinson and Co., 1898), p. 35.

p. 15 "favourite subject": Thompson, *Lark Rise to Candleford*, pp. 229-230.

Chapter 2: The Victorian Village

p. 19 "We went on by": Charles Dickens, *Bleak House* (1851-1853), at http://ebooks.adelaide.edu.au/d/dickens/charles/d54bh/chapter64.html

p. 20 "the spot God made": Thompson, *Lark Rise to Candleford*, p. 279.

p. 21 "should always form part": John Claudius Loudon, *An Encyclopedia of Cottage, Farm, and Villa Architecture and Furniture* (1834); quoted in Souden, *Victorian Village*, p. 30.

p. 23 "a cool and lofty": Hippolyte Taine (1862), quoted in Mingay, *Rural Life in Victorian England*, p. 52.

p. 25 "tenement of, at most": William Howitt, *The Rural Life of England*, vol. 2 (London: Longman, Orme, Brown, Green, and Longmans, 1838), p. 128.

p. 26 "bright and cozy": Thompson, *Lark Rise to Candleford*, p. 4.

p. 27 "At a turn": Francis George Heath, *Peasant Life in the West of England*, 4th ed. (London: Sampson Low, Marston, Searle, and Rivington, 1881), pp. 192-196, 198.

Chapter 3: The Lord of the Manor

p. 29 "Certainly there is": *A Norfolk Diary: Passages from the Diary of the Rev. Benjamin John Armstrong* at www.coxresearcher.com/history/norfolkdiary.htm

p. 29 "Land has ceased": Oscar Wilde, *The Importance of Being Earnest*, Act 1, Part 2 (London: Nick Hern Books, 1995; originally produced 1895), p. 19.

p. 30 "most days of the week": Professor Von Holtzendorff, commenting on the schedule of Barwick Lloyd Baker, squire of Hardwicke Court, Gloucestershire, in 1861; quoted in Ward, *Seasons of Change*, p. 18.

p. 31 "It would be almost": Thompson, *Lark Rise to Candleford*, pp. 209-210.

Chapter 4: The Men of the Farms

p. 37 "Only a man": Thomas Hardy, "In Time of 'The Breaking of Nations'" (1915), at http://www.online-literature.com/hardy/moments-of-vision/149/

p. 39 "If the farming men": William Johnston, *England As It Is*, vol. 1 (London: John Murray, 1851), p. 19.

p. 42 "the hardest graft": An elderly laborer, quoted in Horn, *Labouring Life in the Victorian Countryside*, p. 60.

p. 44 "I saw an old": H. Rider Haggard, *Rural England*, 2nd ed. (London: Longman, 1906); quoted in Mingay, *Rural Life in Victorian England*, p. 83.

p. 45 "reek of the burning": G. P. Pierce, "Village Life in Hampshire," *Hampshire*, February 1962, p. 23; quoted in Horn, *Labouring Life in the Victorian Countryside*, pp. 95-96.

p. 47 "There was hardly": *Royal Commission on Agriculture*, Parliamentary Papers,

1919; quoted in Horn, *Labouring Life in the Victorian Countryside*, p. 107.

CHAPTER 5: THE WOMEN OF THE COUNTRYSIDE

p. 49 "To the women": Thompson, *Lark Rise to Candleford*, p. 275.

p. 49 "The agricultural labourer's": Richard Jefferies, *Hodge and His Masters*, vol. 2 (London: Smith, Elder and Co., 1880), p. 166.

p. 51 "a gang of twelve": Munby Diaries, vol. 16, October 7, 1862, preserved at Trinity College, Cambridge, England; quoted in Horn, *Labouring Life in the Victorian Countryside*, p. 70.

p. 53 "Everything had to be": George Bourne (Sturt), *Change in the Village* (London: George H. Doran, 1912), p. 34.

p. 54 "suspended from their shoulders": Thompson, *Lark Rise to Candleford*, p. 7.

p. 54 "After working": ibid., pp. 274-275.

p. 55 "prepare and cook": Charles Elmé Francatelli, *A Plain Cookery Book for the Working Classes* (Charleston, SC: BiblioBazaar, 2008; originally published 1852), p. 9. A free downloadable copy of this title is available at www.gutenberg.org/ebooks/22114

p. 55 "A lot o' people": A farm laborer, quoted in G. E. Evans, *Where Beards Wag All: The Relevance of the Oral Tradition* (London: Faber and Faber, 1970), pp. 214-215.

p. 55 The recipe for "A Pudding Made of Small Birds" is extracted from Francatelli, *A Plain Cookery Book for the Working Classes*, p. 22.

CHAPTER 6: COUNTRY LADS AND LASSES

p. 57 "Eight appears to be": "Agricultural Gangs," *Quarterly Review* 123 (1867); quoted in Horn, *Labouring Life in the Victorian Countryside*, p. 82.

p. 58 "Jalap pot": Fanny Cowper, quoted in Mabell, Countess of Airlie, *In Whig Society* (London: Hodder and Stoughton, 1921), p. 194.

p. 60 "a little stool": A Norfolk youngster, quoted in Horn, *Labouring Life in the Victorian Countryside*, pp. 155-156.

p. 60 "scarcely more than infants": William Howitt, *The Rural Life of England*, vol. 1 (London: Longman, Orme, Brown, Green, and Longmans, 1838), p. 156.

p. 62 "clean all the Milk Pans": "Reminiscences of Mrs. Florence Davies (née Stowe)" at the Bodleian Library, Oxford, England; quoted in Horn, *Labouring Life in the Victorian Countryside*, pp. 71-72.

p. 65: "When the children": "Some Reasons for the Depopulation of Lincolnshire Villages in the Nineteenth Century by the late Henry Winn of Fulletby," *Lincolnshire Historian* 6, Autumn 1850; quoted in Joan Thirsk, *English Peasant Farming* (London: Routledge, 2006), p. 323.

SOURCES FOR QUOTATIONS

Chapter 7: "All Mirth and Jollity"

p. 67 "When young": Thompson, *Lark Rise to Candleford*, p. 492.

p. 68 "man who labours": Richard Jefferies, *The Toilers of the Field* (London: Longmans, Green, and Co., 1892), p. 100.

p. 68 "good things to eat": "Reminiscences of Mr. Fred Green of Sibford," at Museum of English Rural Life, Reading, England; quoted in Horn, *Labouring Life in the Victorian Countryside*, p. 17.

p. 68 "'Twere all mirth": John Brown of Gloucestershire, quoted in J. Arthur Gibbs, *A Cotswold Village, or Country Life and Pursuits in Gloucestershire* (Whitefish, MT: Kessenger Publishing, 2004; originally published 1918), p. 245.

p. 69 "Nearly every family": Thompson, *Lark Rise to Candleford*, p. 251.

p. 72 "stayed at home": ibid., p. 614.

INDEX

ABOUT THE AUTHOR

VIRGINIA SCHOMP wrote her first short story (starring a magical toad) in kindergarten. She spent the rest of her school years with her nose in a book, pulling it out just long enough to earn a Bachelor of Arts degree in English Literature at Penn State University. Following graduation, she worked at several different publishing companies, learning about the day-to-day details of writing and producing books. After fifteen years of helping other writers realize their dreams, she decided that it was time to become a published writer herself. Since then she has written more than seventy books for young readers on topics including dinosaurs, dolphins, occupations, American history, ancient cultures, and ancient myths. Ms. Schomp lives in the Catskill Mountain region of New York, where she enjoys hiking, gardening, watching old movies on TV and new anime online, and, of course, reading, reading, and reading.